Antony and Cleopatra

A Shakespeare Story

RETOLD BY ANDREW MATTHEWS
ILLUSTRATED BY TONY ROSS

ORCHARD

To Tony and Jean, with love
A.M.

For Oliver K.
T.R.

ORCHARD BOOKS
338 Euston Road, London NW1 3BH
Orchard Books Australia
Hachette Children's Books
Level 17/207 Kent St, Sydney, NSW 2000
This text was first published in Great Britain in the form of a gift collection
called The Orchard Book of Shakespeare Stories, illustrated by
Angela Barrett in 2001.
This edition first published in hardback in Great Britain in 2002
First paperback publication in 2003
This slipcase edition published in 2013
Not for individual resale
Text © Andrew Matthews 2001
Illustrations © Tony Ross 2002
ISBN 978 1 40780 983 0
The rights of Andrew Matthews to be identified as the author and Tony Ross as
the illustrator of this work have been asserted by them in accordance with the
Copyright, Designs and Patents Act, 1988
A CIP catalogue record for this book is available from the British Library
Printed in China

Orchard Books is a division of Hachette Childrens Books,
an Hachette UK company.
www.hachette.co.uk

Contents

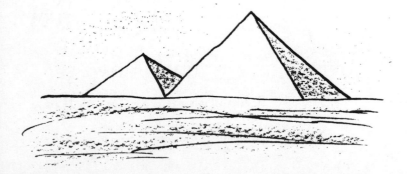

Cast List

Servius
Storyteller
Bodyguard to Antony

Cleopatra
Queen of Egypt

Mark Antony
One of the three rulers of Rome

Octavius Caesar and Lepidus

Rulers of Rome with Antony

Antony's Generals

The Scene

Ancient Egypt and Rome.

Eternity was in our lips and eyes,
Bliss in our brow's bent; none our parts so poor
But was a race of heaven.

Cleopatra; I.iii.

Antony and Cleopatra

You want to know about Antony and Cleopatra? Let me tell you the story – the real story.

I was there at the start, the night Julius Caesar was killed and Antony made a speech over his body in the Market Place.

As soon as Antony stood before us, pale and proud in the torchlight, my heart went out to him. He spoke in a voice like the beating of a war drum, and by the time he had finished speaking, I knew I would follow him anywhere – to the shores of Hades and beyond, if he asked me to.

When civil
war broke out,
I was one of
the first to join
Antony's legions.
It was a bitter,
bloody struggle: Roman
against Roman, each believing that right
was on his side. I was commended for my
courage in action – though
all I did was keep my
head and obey
orders – and
Antony himself
promoted me
to the rank of
centurion, just
before the battle
of Philippi.

That's where I got this scar on my neck,
but I was lucky. Braver men than I died that
day, including Brutus, who killed himself to
escape the shame of defeat. Antony wept at
the sight of Brutus's corpse, and many of us
wept with him.

Then came the peace, though few believed that it would last. The Empire was carved like a goose, and divided up between the three victors. War makes for strange alliances, but none as strange as that trio. Octavius Caesar, Julius Caesar's nephew, was as ruthless and cold as Antony was warm and generous; Lepidus, the third ally, was a joke – a jellyfish with no sting. Caesar took the West, Antony the East, and Lepidus the African provinces that were left over.

11

Almost straight away there was trouble
in the East. The Parthians invaded Roman
territory, and Antony sailed out with his
legions to deal with them. There was a

battle – of sorts. The Parthians were
poorly armed, and undisciplined; most of
them turned and ran the moment they
saw the sunlight shining on our shields.

After the victory, Antony called me to his tent. "Well, Servius," he said, "your centurion days are over."

I thought he was going to pension me off and send me back to Rome. "Why, sir?" I protested.

Antony gave me one of his boyish grins. "Because I want you to join my bodyguard," he said. "I need good fighters about me, men I can trust – and I know I can rely on you."

I was lost for words. My heart beat so proudly that I thought it would burst my armour.

"We leave for Tarsus tonight," Antony said. "I have commanded Queen Cleopatra of Egypt to meet me there, to answer charges that she supplied Brutus with troops and money. I want you at my side. I wouldn't put it past her to slip a hired assassin into the crowds."

"While I've breath in my body, no assassin will get past me to strike at you, sir," I said, and I meant every word.

There was gossip on the road to Tarsus, all of it about Cleopatra, and little of it worth repeating. Men said she was a beauty, who had charmed Julius Caesar and made him fawn over her like a dog. Now, the story went, she planned to do the same with Antony, but I would have none of it. "Caesar was past his prime," I said. "Antony is still young, and his wife is a member of one of Rome's most powerful families. It will take more than some Egyptian woman to make him forget where his loyalty lies, even if she is a queen."

How the Gods must have laughed when they heard that!

A few days later, I was on the quayside at Tarsus with Antony, waiting for Cleopatra's royal barge to arrive. It was more than two hours late, and Antony was annoyed. "This is an insult!" he kept muttering. "That little Nile serpent means to make me look a fool!"

But at last we heard distant voices on the wind: women's voices, singing a twisting, slithering melody that my ears could not follow. Cleopatra's barge rounded a bend in the river, and the watching crowds gasped.

The hull, deck and oars of the barge had

been gilded, so that the boat looked like a
fire burning on the water. The sails were
deep purple and scented and the breeze
that filled them carried the fragrance
across the harbour. I breathed in the
perfume of Egypt for the first time: a spicy,
honeyed smell that made my head swim.

The barge drew close, and I caught my first glimpse of Cleopatra. Her robes were cloth of gold, and she wore the double crown of Egypt. Her skin was golden-brown, her hair black, and glossy as a horse's flank; her huge, dark eyes were deep and still. I had heard tales that Helen of Troy was the most beautiful woman ever, but when I saw Cleopatra, I knew that Helen had been eclipsed.

"This is no Queen!" Antony said softly.
"This is a Goddess!"

Cleopatra stepped onto the quay, and
the cheering crowds sounded like storm
waves breaking.

Antony stepped forward and said, "In the name of the Senate and People of Rome, I greet you, and require you to..." He broke off in astonishment as Cleopatra knelt at his feet and bowed her head.

The crowds fell silent.

Antony frowned, then bent down, and helped Cleopatra to her feet. "My noble lord does me too much honour," she said, her head still lowered.

"There is much to discuss," said Antony, "but this is not a fit place. Dine with me tonight, in the city."

"No, my lord,"
Cleopatra said.

'No' was not
a word that
Antony was used
to hearing, and I saw
him stiffen in anger; but
then Cleopatra looked up at him. "Dine
with me, on the barge," she said. "Let me
see if my Egyptian cooks can please you.
Eat with me and taste new
delights, my lord."

Antony looked
into Cleopatra's
eyes, and his
anger melted.

"Now I am
the honoured
one," he said.

I knew then that he had fallen in love with her, as surely as if I had seen one of Eros's arrows pierce his heart.

Within a week, we set sail for Egypt, and nothing was ever the same again.

***

Egypt was another world. Beyond the
Nile's green valley stretched the desert,
unchanging and timeless. In Egypt, the
years slipped away like a handful of water.

Antony grew older and softer. He seemed to care for nothing but Cleopatra and their children. Some of the soldiers became restless, saying that Antony was not the man he had once been, and that Cleopatra had bewitched him. Such talk made me angry. "You'll see Antony's greatness again when the time comes!" I said.

And the time came. There was chaos in Rome: Antony's wife, Fulvia, and Lucius, his brother, raised an army to overthrow Octavius Caesar and were crushed in battle. Fulvia died on her way to see Antony in Egypt.

At the same time, Sextus Pompeius rebelled against Caesar, and the Parthians invaded the Roman territories at their borders.

The world of Rome seemed about to collapse.

I was with Antony when the dispatches reached him. His face darkened as he read them, and for a long time he brooded in silence. "Is it true, Servius?" he asked at last. "Am I really as old and weak as they say?"

"You are Mark Antony, sir," I told him.

Something of his old look shone in Antony's eyes. "I will go to Rome and settle my differences with Caesar," he said. "If he, I and Lepidus make peace with Pompeius, we can put our forces together, defeat the Parthians and save Rome before it is too late." Then his face fell. "But what shall I tell the Queen?" he murmured.

Cleopatra stormed, and wept and
pleaded, but at last she saw that she had
no choice but to let Antony go. She feared
he would not return, but I knew that his
love for her was too strong for him to
keep away for very long.

* * *

In Rome, Antony was a grizzled lion,

Caesar a cold and haughty eagle,

and Lepidus a crab, scurrying beside them.

They talked behind locked doors, late into the night and standing guard outside, I heard Antony and Caesar raise their voices in anger, while Lepidus twittered and whined.

Antony emerged from the chamber looking tired and worried. He took me aside and said, "I want you to leave for Egypt at once. Tell the Queen that I have made my peace with Caesar."

I frowned: this was good news – yet Antony's face was troubled.

"But the peace came at a price," he went on. "To strengthen the alliance, I must marry Octavia, Caesar's sister. Tell the Queen that the marriage means nothing, and that my love for her is unchanged. I will return to Egypt with Octavia when we have signed a treaty with Pompeius."

Doubts rose
in my mind
like a flock of
crows. All
Rome knew
how dearly
Caesar loved
his sister. How
long would it be
before he
discovered that her
marriage to Antony was a sham? It would
be all the excuse he needed to declare war
and try to seize the whole Empire for
himself. And when Cleopatra heard of the
marriage, who could tell what she might
do? I glimpsed Antony's future, and it was
all blood and shadows.

✳ ✳ ✳

I had no flowery words to decorate Antony's message. I spoke out like a soldier, blunt and plain.

Cleopatra's rage was furious. "Tell me that you are lying, or you shall be whipped with wire and boiled in salted water!" she shrieked.

"Madam, I speak the truth," I said. "Antony is married to Octavia." Cleopatra drew a knife; I do not know whether she intended to stab me or herself, for one of her handmaidens snatched the knife away. Cleopatra shook her head, scattering tears that gleamed as they fell. "Then let Egypt sink into the Nile!" she moaned. "Let the sky fall and crush the Earth!"

Egypt did not sink, nor did the sky fall, but one terrible happening led to another.

Before Antony and Octavia were halfway to Egypt, Caesar broke the treaty with Pompeius, defeated him in battle, seized the African provinces and had Lepidus put to death. Antony knew that war was coming, and sent Octavia back to Rome, being too honourable a man to keep her as a hostage.

Once Antony was back in Egypt,
he and Cleopatra joined forces against
Caesar. Though their love remained
strong, some of the fire between them
had dwindled because of Antony's
marriage of convenience.

Antony seemed his old self again, confident and decisive; but also headstrong, as if age had made him stubborn instead of wise. Against all advice, he insisted on a battle at sea, to prevent Caesar from landing his troops.

Antony's generals were in despair. "This is madness, sir!" one of them was brave enough to tell him. "The enemy ships greatly outnumber ours. If we lose the fleet, we cannot keep our troops supplied. Fight Caesar on land!"

"Let no man say that Antony feared to face an enemy," Antony replied. "I will meet Caesar at sea!"

Actium, they called that battle. I still dream of it, and wake up shouting. The ships fired flaming pitch and sulphur at one another. Burning men leapt screaming

into the sea and when two ships came
alongside, soldiers from each tried to
board the other, so the decks ran red.

For a time, it seemed that Antony might
be victorious; then love betrayed him.
Cleopatra sailed out in her barge, thinking
that the sight of her would encourage
Antony and the Egyptian fleet; but the
horror and slaughter of the battle made
her order the barge back to harbour.

A Roman galley broke formation to give chase, and Antony turned his ship around to go to Cleopatra's rescue. When the captains of the fleet saw their commander leave the fight, they believed that all was lost, and fled.

After the disaster at Actium, Antony bargained for peace. He offered Caesar his third of the Empire, in return for being allowed to stay in Egypt with the Queen.

Caesar refused: he would make peace with Cleopatra, he said, but only if Antony were executed.

Antony accused Cleopatra of betraying him, out of spite for his marriage to Octavia. Cleopatra was terrified by Antony's fury, and went into hiding.

The generals had their land battle in the end – outside the walls of Alexandria. We fought like heroes, and Caesar's men fell like wheat to the scythe. But even as the celebrations began in Antony's tent, a messenger arrived with grave news. The Egyptian fleet had surrendered; Antony could no longer keep his army fed and armed; the war was lost.

Antony ordered everyone from the tent, except me. When we were alone, he drew his sword and offered it to me, hilt first.

"Kill me, Servius," he said. "I cannot bear to beg Caesar for mercy."

"Sir," I said, "I know where the Queen is hiding. You could be with her in an hour. You could escape to…"

"To live in fear until Caesar hunts us down?" said Antony. "No, Servius. I am finished. Take the sword and end it."

"Not I, sir!" I said. "I would gladly die for you, but I will not do what you ask."

"Then by my own hand be it," said Antony.

He stabbed with both hands, but the point of the sword slipped on his breastbone and ran into his belly. He pulled out the sword and threw it across the tent with a cry of disgust, knowing that his death would be long and painful. Agony drove him to his knees. "Cleopatra!" he gasped. "Take me to her!"

*** *** ***

I do not know how Antony found the strength to stand, and mount a horse, but as night fell we rode across the desert to Cleopatra's hiding place: her own tomb, built in the shape of a crouching lion with a man's head. I beat against the doors, my shouts echoing off the stone, until a slave answered, and drew back the bolts. Antony leaned on me, and we staggered inside.

The tomb was lit by a hundred oil lamps that shone on the richly decorated walls. Paintings of Egyptian Gods stared down with sightless, animal eyes. Cleopatra was seated on a throne, dressed in her royal robes. A reed basket stood at her feet, and I remember thinking it a poor thing to find in such a place.

Cleopatra saw the blood from Antony's wound, and ran to him. We gently laid him down. Cleopatra sat, and rested his head on her lap.

"I am dying, Egypt," Antony said. "Tell Caesar you had me killed, and make peace with him."

"Never!" said Cleopatra.

Antony's face clenched in pain. "Then add one more kiss to the thousands you have given me," he said.

Cleopatra lowered her head, pressed her lips to Antony's, and he was gone.

"The sun has burned out," Cleopatra whispered. "The world is dark."

Tears clouded
my eyes. I did
not see the
Queen stand,
or reach into
the basket and
take out the small
black snake coiled within it.

When I could see again, she was on her
throne, and the snake's
fangs were sunk deep
in her breast.
"Sweet as perfume!"
she said. "Soft
as air! Oh,
Antony!"

And so her
life ended.

* * *

And that's my story. It will be told and retold, until time ends. Antony and Cleopatra will always be together, though their beauty and greatness turned to desert dust long ago.

They say that in the East, Emperor Octavius Caesar is worshipped as a God. Well, if Caesar is a God, then let my death come soon, for the world is past my understanding.

But Antony – now there was a man!

She shall be buried by her Antony.
No grave upon the earth shall clip in it
A pair so famous.

Caesar; V.ii.

Love and Death in
Antony and Cleopatra

When Mark Antony and Cleopatra meet, they both know that they have found the love of their lives.

Antony is a Roman, a disciplined soldier, and a courageous and brilliant general who rules a third of the Roman Empire. Queen Cleopatra of Egypt is beautiful, stubborn, fiery-tempered and used to having her own way. Yet in spite of their differences, Antony's love for Cleopatra is so strong that he abandons Rome and stays in Egypt, where they live together and have several children.

Then history turns against them. In order to keep the Roman world united, Antony is forced to marry the sister of Octavius Caesar. The marriage is a sham and Antony quickly returns to Egypt, but this gives the ambitious Octavius the excuse he needs to make war and take the whole empire for himself.

Against the advice of his generals, Antony fights the Roman fleet at Actium, where Cleopatra's meddling causes a massive defeat. Antony bungles a suicide attempt and is taken to Cleopatra's hiding place. He dies in her arms.

Antony sacrifices everything for Cleopatra – his reputation, his loyalty to his country, and his life. After he is dead, Octavius offers Cleopatra peace, but she chooses a noble death over a shameful surrender. Cleopatra cannot bear to live without Antony and joins him in death, passing out of history into legend, where her and Antony's love will live for ever.

Shakespeare and the Globe Theatre

Some of Shakespeare's most famous plays were first performed at the Globe Theatre, which was built on the South Bank of the River Thames in 1599.

Going to the Globe was a different experience from going to the theatre today. The building was roughly circular in shape, but with flat sides: a little like a doughnut crossed with a fifty-pence piece. Because the Globe was an open-air theatre, plays were only put on during daylight hours in spring and summer. People paid a penny to stand in the central space and watch a play, and this part of the audience became known as 'the groundlings' because they stood on the ground. A place in the tiers of seating beneath the thatched roof, where there was a slightly better view and less chance of being rained on, cost extra.

The Elizabethans did not bath very often and the audiences at the Globe were smelly. Fine ladies and gentlemen in the more expensive seats sniffed perfume and bags of sweetly-scented herbs to cover the stink rising from the groundlings.

There were no actresses on the stage; all the female characters in Shakespeare's plays would have been acted by boys, wearing wigs and make-up. Audiences were not well-behaved. People clapped and cheered when their favourite actors came on stage; bad actors were jeered at and sometimes pelted with whatever came to hand.

Most Londoners worked hard to make a living and in their precious free time they liked to be entertained. Shakespeare understood the magic of the theatre so well that today, almost four hundred years after his death, his plays still cast a spell over the thousands of people that go to see them.

Orchard Classics
Shakespeare Stories

RETOLD BY ANDREW MATTHEWS
ILLUSTRATED BY TONY ROSS

As You Like It	978 1 84616 187 2	£4.99
Hamlet	978 1 84121 340 8	£4.99
A Midsummer Night's Dream	978 1 84121 332 3	£4.99
Antony and Cleopatra	978 1 84121 338 5	£4.99
The Tempest	978 1 84121 346 0	£4.99
Richard III	978 1 84616 185 8	£4.99
Macbeth	978 1 84121 344 6	£4.99
Twelfth Night	978 1 84121 334 7	£4.99
Henry V	978 1 84121 342 2	£4.99
Romeo & Juliet	978 1 84121 336 1	£4.99
Much Ado About Nothing	978 1 84616 183 4	£4.99
Othello	978 1 84616 184 1	£4.99
Julius Caesar	978 1 40830 506 5	£4.99
King Lear	978 1 40830 503 4	£4.99
The Merchant of Venice	978 1 40830 504 1	£4.99
The Taming of the Shrew	978 1 40830 505 8	£4.99

Orchard Books are available from all good bookshops.